Art with children

Art with children

Daphne Plaskow

Studio Vista London
Watson-Guptill Publications New York

Acknowledgements

I should like to acknowledge the support and encouragement in my work which I have received from the Society for Education through Art. Among individuals to whom I owe thanks are Maggie Macgregor, whose nursery playgroup is an inspiration; the Hersham Infants' School and Mrs Maclarty; Oatlands Junior School, Mrs Hall and Miss Donald; and the Chobham Infants' School and Mrs Hodgson. The photographs Figs. 61, 84, 85, 89, 91, 101, 102a, 103 and 114 are by Simon Carrier; the jacket photograph is by Michael Holford.

My greatest debt of gratitude is to my three children, whose creative activity provide the incentive for writing this book.

© Daphne Plaskow 1968
Published in London by Studio Vista Limited
Blue Star House, Highgate Hill, London N 19
and in New York by Watson-Guptill Publications
165 West 46th Street, New York 10036
Distributed in Canada by General Publishing Co. Ltd
30 Lesmill Road, Don Mills, Toronto, Ontario
Library of Congress Catalog Card Number 68-13120
Set in Univers 9 on 10 point
by V. Siviter Smith & Co. Ltd, Birmingham
Printed and bound in Great Br' ain

SBN 289 37045 0

Contents

Fig. 1

Introduction

The first part of the book gives an outline of the stages every child seems to go through in his art work, so that it should be possible to identify your child within his relevant age-group section. Suggestions are given for creative things to do at all ages and step by step accounts of how to do them are arranged alphabetically in Part Two.

Why should children paint? Why should any child want to spend his time making things out of scraps, or hacking shapes out of block salt, or hammering nails into a block of wood, or doing big drawings with felt tipped pens? From the moment when a child first puts his fingers round a pencil or brush and finds that he can make a mark with it, he searches for encouragement and praise from adults. Why should he get it, for the production of nothing but scribble? Because this first effort is more than scribble; the marks he makes are a valuable part of his growth and development and he needs your help with it.

Through the holding of a pencil or brush the small child learns to use muscles in hand and arm not used before, particularly the tiny gripping muscles in the hand. As he becomes aware that a mark appears on his paper when he applies pressure and moves the instrument, he learns to become the master of the marks he makes. This enormous step forward in development is natural to all children who are given the opportunity. It takes place at any stage from about a year old, and can take hours, days or perhaps weeks to achieve.

Just the simple recognition that he has made a mark himself is a happy and proud moment for a toddler. The odds are that his discovery comes at a time when he has not yet learnt words or even sounds to transmit exactly what he feels—these new lines, and possibly colours if he is allowed to paint, are to be his way of communicating for a very long time. Possibly until his command of language is very good his pictures will look scribbly, but into them he will put all his emotions of the moment for you to read. Children thrive on praise. To encourage by saying how very fine a picture is, or 'what a lovely drawing' cannot possibly indulge him. And it's a two-way process. One wants to please one's child and to detect and encourage any talent he might show. He will not understand the words if he is tiny, but the tone of voice will please him by making him feel that whatever he is doing is

Fig. 2

obviously giving pleasure to the adult he loves, and that to perpetuate this he should do more of it.

At the different stages of development in the child there will be similar need for encouragement, praise, and sometimes stimulus from grown-ups. Once a child can communicate in speech, the things he paints or draws or makes with his hands will change in content and character. Just as one needs an adequate command of words before one can explore the deeper sensitivity of poetry, so must the child become familiar with what he can do with line, with brush, with colour. When he is at pre-school age he may go on to probe deeper into more emotional fields, by not drawing mummy, daddy and the baby

Fig. 3

any more, but depicting things that have happened to him, or even imaginary situations. The nursery school child I know who painted 'my garden and there's a fairy down there and she comes out at night and makes the flowers grow' is an example; and a small boy's drawing of 'Ian downstairs chasing the monsters who are trying to eat him' is another: a piece of fantasy lived out on paper and by it rendered harmless.

Stages of development

All children think from themselves outwards to their surroundings; the tiny child draws mummy and daddy, any other children, the

9

Elizabeth with Nicola

Fig. 4

dog, the house, and the car, often in that order. However, as he develops in the warmth and encouragement of his family circle, he has the self-confidence to look outward to other people or things which influence his emotional life, for he is a creature of emotion, not yet able to rationalise or order his thoughts.

Obviously when he starts going to school, at five or six, he will be learning to organise his actions, and will begin a perhaps difficult process of adjustment to a larger unit than the family. His creative activity, his painting and modelling, may then be as important to him as an outlet, as at any other time in his life, and the solidarity expressed by his family or teacher by their encouragement may help him at least to give vent to his emotions—at most to arrange his thoughts.

10

Fig. 5

Fig. 6

Fig. 7

Fig. 8   Fig. 9

For about the first three years of school, work is not divided into subjects; the learning process is a play or discovery situation. Within that time the child grows and alters physically, and learns to read and calculate in a class with other children. In many schools he will also be given the opportunity to draw and paint, model and carve, expressing new experiences, defining, describing and making his discoveries intensified through his work. When a small boy paints a red motor-bicycle, as he paints the red and the motor-bicycle he understands both more than before, each enters his experience and becomes, so to speak, part of his visual vocabulary. He rolls out his first snakes of clay and coils them into plate or pot, getting the fulsome feeling of the clay squishing through his fingers, gradually becoming smoother, yet soft and manageable. The roundness of a good pot, the texture as it dries, will become a part of his experience. The first three years or so of school are the time when the child, seeing more of the outside world and given the opportunity to draw and paint it,

12

Fig. 10

13

will develop a keener understanding as his awareness grows. At this time parents and teachers can 'read' the paintings of children, associating them with what they know of the children through previous pictures and everyday contact.

One can, as a parent, gain a great deal of insight into the child and his feelings about things, from what he does in his pictures, and from his general attitude to his art work. Sometimes a child has fears which can be expressed in pictures: fear of the dark, fear of animals of some kind, fear of crossing the road, or just a simple fear of getting dirty, which could show itself by his opting out of making or painting anything. For anything we can learn about our children in this way — about things which they repress, but which we can unobtrusively set about putting to rights — we should be glad; as we are, of course, when we glean information of a useful kind from other 'second-hand' sources.

The role of the parent

However, any message or meaning which children's art may contain is usually greatest for the people who know the children best. They can see the importance of the work in the child's development, which is where the product counts most. The child himself healthily disregards the work he does when he has grown to a stage of doing things better; this means that all those models from last week can go off the shelf today, if he has been free to make more models which may be better. In the home situation, and particularly the small home or flat, creative children create problems as well as good art work, but informed and enthusiastic parents can see that as a child develops and outgrows one toy in favour of another, so his art needs will change too. The stages he goes through may mean perhaps different sizes of paper and brushes, different paper too. A careful line drawing in ink needs better paper than the five-year-old's wrapping paper daubs, for example.

There are still terrible misconceptions, however about whether to encourage children to create things at home if it is felt that they have no talent. It must be emphasised that the freedom to develop emotionally in artistic creativity is the due of all children, and anything creative and imaginative that any child can be encouraged to do will help him to discover values of all kinds.

A most important function of all parents is to develop the child, not to develop a talent; talent is a natural predisposition to

14

the job in hand, not necessarily life's vocation, its' existence is an indication that people have been encouraging and that things have gone right. Talent in all children appears to grow from something they have done which was above average and was singled out for praise and encouragement. To this extent then, the field is wide open for any child to develop a sense that his work is good and that adults feel that it is important to continue with it.

Fig. 11

Fig. 12 A two year-old's picture of 'pussy'

1 The early years

Scribbling

The tiny child grabs a crayon, waves it in every direction – it makes marks all over the place. The simple pleasure of holding, moving the crayon up and down or round and getting scribbles is now contributing to the development of tiny hand muscles and motor control; this can take weeks or months. But not long after marks begin to be controlled the adult can start to talk to the toddler about what he is drawing. At first, a two year-old just beginning to draw, might find the idea of representation strange. 'Is it a drawing of mummy – or the kitten – or the house?' could be met with a bewildered repetitive reply. This could be because the toddler is not yet ready for the suggestion; but quite soon, as the child scribbles and talks, a sort of drawing play emerges. Maybe he sees a similarity between something in his thought and in his drawing, and he starts to identify the lines with things in his experience. It is impossible to say where the power to identify begins in the small child. For some time within this new stage, he will babble about the pictures he is doing, and on going back to an early one will be found to have forgotten the original identification. So, when a child is just beginning, one should encourage his imaginary play in pictures, because what he is doing is teaching himself to think.

Talking about the paintings or pictures will encourage the child to go on and do more. It is important that, even if the scribbles look quite unlike anything at all, the child should not be told so, but should be encouraged to talk by 'tell me about it,' or 'that's a lovely part.'

Growing out of scribble

From the baby stage of gripping a crayon to making controlled marks, then undecipherable scribbles which the small child can identify, he goes on to another stage, a development from the previous one, where things are at last more recognisable. Round scribbles are now perhaps 'the sun, and it's shining down on us', or 'it's the car, and I'm going out for a ride'. This begins to be a little more encouraging, because the poor parent need now make

Figs. 13 and 14

fewer mistakes in identification. By now the child himself is more sure as to exactly what his pictures are about; this is a stage of putting down things he himself knows very well or has been excited by. A wonderful trip to the circus, interesting days at the sea, meeting daddy from the train (as long as they all take place within the family), will be the typical motivating experience at this time.

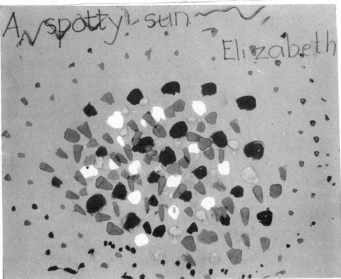

Fig. 17 *A Spotty Sun*

The more the child is helped by conversation to think about the experience the deeper his feeling about it will tend to be, although one has to be careful that the child should not feel that the adult has taken over. To be harried by too many questions might stop him working entirely, but suggestions like 'do you remember the clown's baggy trousers, and his enormous shoes?' might at least prove your interest in his circus picture and start him talking about other exciting facts he remembers.

At this time, which is usually when the child is around three years old, he will use any intense experience as a stimulus. There are great variations, at this baby level, in the ages where these

Figs. 13 and 14 On the previous page
Figs. 15 and 16 Opposite, are the work of three, four and five year-olds

This clowns
name is
coco.

This mans name
is Robin-hood.

These Clowns are very funny
funny clowns

Figs. 18, 19 and 20 These crayon drawings are part of a small book made of writing pad after a visit to the circus. The artist was five and a half years old.

different stages will occur, and really it does not matter much when the small child goes through them, early or late, either from his point of view or that of his parents. The child will progress through the stages of muscular control, and later, identification within an imaginary play situation, as these are essential to his development, although he may stay only a short time in one and longer in another.

Tools for the job

Scribbling can be an arduous task for a small child if he hasn't the right things to do it with. Ideally one should try to provide materials which are right for the child by allowing him to choose for himself from a range of large wax crayons, big brushes and felt tipped pens. If it is not possible, even in a shop, to allow a child to select what he wants, it is important when he is beginning that he should have wax crayons or brushes which are thick enough to give him something to hold. An overlong brush can be a nuisance; a stubby one with fairly rigid bristles is ideal. A very good drawing marker can be made from a piece of half-inch dowel about six inches long, split at one end with a tool, held open to take a small lump of plastic foam which is held firmly when the split is released. All kinds of these markers can be made, to produce different kinds of lines, dependent on the fabric used. Carpet felt cut into strips, or plastic draught-proofing strip are both good holders of paint or ink when they are rolled

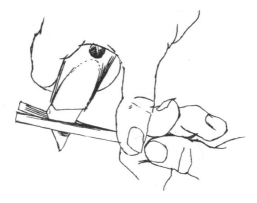

Fig. 21 Making a drawing stick. Slit the end of your stick, and insert a small wad of foam rubber or other texture. The springiness of the stick should hold the fabric, but secure with a rubber band if necessary.

lightly and inserted into the split to leave a brush-size ball of fabric to work with.

It is important also that this age group should use things that work. The frustration of the paint pot gone dry, or wax crayon

Fig. 22   Fig. 23

that slides off the paper without making a mark, are not for the young child, who would suddenly rather go and play with his engine.

For painting, only very few colours are needed—say three or four at most. A jar of poster colour costs very little. A tin of powdered colour (ready to mix with water) about six inches high can be bought for even less. Whenever needed, a new mix of powder paint and water can be made in the bottom of a yoghourt container—only a little, for a child gets great pleasure from coming up for more. This is perhaps the cheapest method of providing good dense-coloured paint for small children. A modest amount for paints plus the price of dowel gives one materials to last for months.

Paper is not a problem with this age group, for young children will paint on newspaper, wrapping paper and even flattened-out paper bags, if the budget will not run to sugar paper (construction paper) or the more expensive grades of cartridge (white drawing paper). Shelf lining paper can be bought in rolls, which is economical as it can be cut to the size the child wants as he uses it; but it goes bumpy and makes puddles when too watery paint is used, so it must be used with newspaper underneath.

So, with a supply of newspaper, marker brushes and paint in

22

yoghourt containers, the child is all set. Each container should have a brush of its own—or a homemade marker—so that no water need be used for brush cleaning. That is a function the tiny child does not understand anyway, and the water inevitably finds its way over the child, the table and the floor. The child will need an overall or a smock, such as a shirt put on backwards or a soft plastic apron. Painting overalls can be bought for children at most stores, but the plastic or rubber should be soft, not crackly, or the child will be unable to move freely. The table and the floor can be protected by decorative plastic or vinyl fabric, (which can be bought by the yard), by shower or bathroom curtaining, or by decorators' plastic sheeting which can be bought in stock sizes.

Ideally, painting or messy jobs performed by the child should be done where a little splashing can be mopped up easily afterwards, say in a tiled kitchen, or in the garage. Where that is not possible newspaper or plastic on the floor should help inspire confidence in the child that he can now do what he wants, rather than make him inhibited and unable to brush a stroke. Put him in the bathroom to paint rather than give him a too-tidy complex at this stage.

Suitable materials for the scribbler are referred to on page 73 of Part Two. Small children draw, mostly with crayons, paint, or homemade drawing markers; see pages 21 and 85.

Fig. 24 A two year-old ready to paint

Fig. 25

3 Nursery school

When control comes naturally, within the nursery school age group, there is less need to caution about mess. If the early stages of painting are handled without upset, later stages come easily, the child fitting into a now established pattern. He knows where his overall is, where sheeting is for the table, lays out his paper and has only to ask to get paints mixed.

Drawing and painting in the nursery school age group is a marvellously spontaneous activity, and very enjoyable for both parent and teacher. No special stimulus need be given as once the child has achieved a confidence in his drawing and handling of paint he begins a stage of outpouring. This self-expression in paint is a valuable communication to parent and teacher who are keen to understand the child in this period of rapid physical and mental development. He is now identifying himself in the world around him as he sees it.

Almost throughout a child's development the 'I', 'me', 'my', is either there or implied in his picture-making; but it is most obvious with the four to six year-old. *Me, My Mummy, Me on the Bus, Riding my Tricycle;* these are the sorts of pictures which appear early in this period. Children have to feel and know their subjects well before they put anything down, and tend to start being representational with pictures of the family, the house, the car, the sun and the flowers. Where a picture contains all those elements, the family will be big—perhaps with mummy biggest of all—the house smaller, the car smaller still, and so on.

Most of the pictures of four to six year-olds contain human beings, because they are just learning to be outgoing, new experiences and sensations are being taken in all the time. Eventually, through self-expressive activities at this nursery stage, the small child learns to control and select, and simplify what he sees and feels.

Fig. 26

Now the child can produce drawings which contain very similar shapes, circles with features, box shapes, sun shapes, but which can be altered fractionally to depict something quite different. A four-legged dog can become an eight or ten-legged caterpillar; a house with wheels and an elongated front becomes the family car; the sun becomes the baby with the addition of two legs. In a few minutes one can see a picture change completely by a few 'minor' details. The imagination of a child is sufficient to carry him from one pictorial experience to another so quickly.

Even while he is so young, the child may already have a recognisable style, which will have evolved in the course of his work. One child may be neat and controlled, never smearing colours and mixing them on the paper another may prefer to draw with large bold sweeps.

Figs. 27 and 28 Sculpture made of sections of cardboard tube of different widths

Variety adds spice

With children of up to six years old, it is essential not only to provide materials, but also to help them appreciate things they might not necessarily regard as important. Smoothness, roughness of texture and pattern surround them all the time, but are not always noticed. Children can make rubbings on paper of brickwork, tree bark, tiles, manhole covers and so on and could make a big collage from these scraps of texture rubbing (see pages 68 and 102). They enjoy experimenting, especially with varieties of papers, which can usually be stuck fast with any of the heavier glues. Cellophane, coloured tissue, gift or sweet wrapping papers, silver paper or aluminium foil, corrugated paper, might all be collected into a cardboard box in the child's room, so that over a period a supply is accumulated to make his final picturemaking choice as wide as possible. Often some unusual piece of texture or colour will spark off a wonderful innovation. At this stage, however, the resulting picture should not be thought to matter too much. If it looks a mess it may still be that some order out of the chaos has been achieved by the child. It is the process, not the end product, which counts.

Fig. 29 Collage called *The Old House*, using fabric, cut paper, an earring, dried melon seeds, and cut-outs of prints of textures. See also pages 68-69.

Particularly at the six year-old end of this group it is useful to be able to model, in clay, plasticine, clay flour (powdered clay to which water is added), or in the new clayola, (which is plasticine, but without the distinctive smell). Even tiny three year-olds like to bang plasticine: take precautions, because if it is walked into a carpet it can be disastrous. Clay can be bought by weight from large toy shops already made up in plastic bags; clayola and clay flour are made up from powder, as needed and are obtainable from art suppliers or educational firms.

As muscles develop and more hand control is attained, children's metal scissors with rounded ends can be introduced. Infant school teachers say that doing up buttons and cutting with scissors are the two most difficult things for a child to do at the time of entering school, so a little help might be useful. Collages, made of cutout shapes of coloured sticky paper could combine cutting and sticking with perhaps painting or drawing on top.

Three dimensional creations, such as hobby-horses made with socks, or dachshunds, or enormous worms made from stockings, can be embellished beautifully with bottle-top spots, bits of foil, tissue paper flowers, string hair, etc., attached with strong vegetable glue or perhaps a bodkin (a blunt needle) and thread.

Masks made from paper plates, with suitable features either painted or made from stuck on pieces of egg-boxes, with some invention for hair, can carry through a child's idea in a picture. 'Let's make a mask of the postman' could be an interesting follow-up to a painting.

Pre-school age children like to draw and paint (see pages 73 and 85), to model with plasticine and clay (page 81), and to stick and cut out all sorts of textures (page 102). Paper and fabrics are used to make collages (page 68) also puppets and toys (page 77).

Fig. 30

Fig. 31 *The Blue Caterpillar*

4 The six to nine year-olds

The years between six and nine see an enormous growth in the children's interests and abilities, and also, occasionally, a surprising incompatibility between what they would like to achieve and what they can actually do. Surprising because they are now at a stage where they can do so much, socially. It is a stage, too, where children vary in their attitudes. A child who, until starting at primary, or elementary school, has been very productive, always at work, may seem now to have switched permanently to television, the more rumbustious comics, and the Saturday film-shows. Another child who seemed to have no particular creative interest before becomes a collector of stones and geological finds and begs and swaps for a stamp collection.

During this age-span children are very susceptible to adults' attitudes, drawing on them largely as a basis for their own. The six year-old has built up a standard of behaviour which 'goes' at home. The way he reacts, now that he has reached the age of compulsory school may show that he needs to do something creative – painting or building.

Fig. 32

Fig. 33

The rules of the game

Children have to develop through different stages in their art work. The six to nine year-old has reached a period with rigid conventions and ways of depicting reality, as the child understands it.

At this time a child is working things out; relationships of all kinds, emotions, size, colour. It is probably simpler for him to establish these if he develops motifs for the object used most in his pictures. The figure, which used to be so variable, is now standardised — to each child his own individual theme, which he repeats again and again, varying the details, but always using the same main formula. The figure, for example, may be dressed in clothes, instead of merely having a body; there may be arms straight out sideways, with fingers (any number), coming out of the sleeves. There is a set way of drawing eyes, noses and mouths, so that each feature will look the same on all figures.

The second most obvious change that comes with this period is that the ground on which all the figures stand in the picture will be the bottom of the page, and the sky a blue streak across the top. Birds cling upside down to the skyline — 'birds are in the sky, aren't they'? Trucks race along the ground line in a similarly reasonable way. Everything has its place. The action being shown can then be put into the space between ground and sky (fig. 35).

Fig. 34

When one understands the child's individual simplifications one can go further towards understanding him by means of observing the deviations that he sometimes makes from these simplifications. When a child does something different from usual—changes the expression on a face, draws a tree quite differently, exaggerates or distorts something, it can be regarded

Fig. 35 *Gathering Apples*

as significant. His realisation of what he has seen, his awareness of whatever it is he has shown, has developed so that he now understands something new about it. In the picture the man's arm looks to be six feet long and the hand as big as a baseball mitt. The child has felt the extension of that arm reaching out to catch the ball, and the all-important catching hand will have

Fig. 36 Detail from a larger drawing showing exaggeration

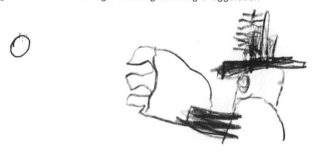

grown put of scale in the emotion of the moment. Something has been experienced all the time in the creative work of our children, though we may not all be aware of it.

This age group uses other set formulae as well. There is an aerial photograph way of showing people, in a swimming pool for example, the rectangle of the pool in the centre of the page, the swimmers flat across it, while onlookers, their feet on the borders of the pool stretch round the picture like the spokes of a wheel. A road across the paper might have houses bordering it on both sides, flat to the sides of the road; a road uphill might have trees along it, but always at 90° to the line of the road, not to the line of the paper.

There is an X-ray, diagrammatic way of showing action going on within a shape, whether a building or an animal. A house can be shown almost as a cutaway, some parts being the accepted outside, but others quite obviously showing the interior with furniture, the stairs, and smoke going up the chimney. Occasionally a child may draw several ground lines with things going on at each level, rather like a comic strip, or like ancient Egyptian writing.

Fig. 37 *Simon's Mummy*. This pre-school child found out the function of a nose and painted this picture to record the discovery

I make my own rules

A child of the six to nine age group is not at his best working with others, for his method is still such an individual matter. Group learning and working on pictures with other children is often unsuccessful at this time, as very little is achieved in the way of a personal statement from the child. The temptation to help children get proportions 'right', adding a bit of perspective to achieve realism, is a negative approach and should be resisted. Any progress a child makes in art as well as in terms of emotional experience he has to make for himself. The portrait (fig. 37) is a case in point. In the morning, before going to school, the child had become aware of his nose, his nostrils and their function. It was such a deep realisation to him that when at school he immediately painted the portrait, directly with a brush, thereby making a mental note for ever. This does not necessarily mean that he will ever after paint noses in this way, simply that now that he has realised the existence of a nose he may observe this feature more closely in future.

Fig. 39

An important characteristic of this time is that the formulae children use are constantly changing with their growing awareness. As soon as a feature becomes meaningful to them it will be expressed differently. The intelligent child will never be satisfied for long with a generalised statement. The overall look of the child's work appears to change as an indication that he is inquiring into the detail, not content with his work as it is.

The drawing of the wild west sharpshooter, (fig. 39) by a six year-old, shows that the artist has been intrigued by the guns in the holster, a deviation from the usual theme; it would seem, however, that he meant the drawing to be a portrait because there is no distorted action here. Cowboy and horse have a sense of belonging to each other—even looking a little alike—because the noses are drawn in exactly the same way, and the faces are the same shape. The child's inquiry into the details of horse and cowboy have been limited almost entirely to the guns, otherwise the drawing is only an emotion of wild west, probably triggered off by television.

However, the drawing *I am a Fireman*, drawn by the same boy only a week or so after the cowboy and horse, depicts something with which the boy identifies, and knows much more about.

36

Television, a sequence of moving pictures, leaves a small child with a blurred emotion and little awareness of detail. As a result there is little or no identification with the television situation when the child is immature, and he achieves very little meaningful stimulus from it in terms of self development. The drawing of the fireman, however, with his helmet, buttons, tunic and boots, although not apparently full of action, has a much better observed figure than the other drawing. The figure is running, and the legs are therefore distorted in length: this is typical of the formula for running, the legs seen from a side view and the distorted length—but there is observation too in the interesting angle of the feet. Perhaps this fireman is the driver. The engine bell is clanging but the wheels are not moving, and the cabin is out-lined carefully as if to establish a link between figure and machine. The bows on the boots are an intriguing detail, but are an auto-matic mark made on all other footwear in earlier drawings by the same child.

Help! I need somebody

Your child will almost certainly ask for help at some time between the ages of six and nine. School may be good for him if it uses discovery and experience techniques, but even in that case there may be questions relating to him personally to which he needs answers. If you can help him discover the answers he may still be painting at nine. Periods of inactivity follow obstructions in the child's development, and those can be so simple. When a child is 'stuck' he may use one theme time and time again, each picture saying no more than the last. When this happens, take

Fig. 40 *Fireman and Fire Engine*

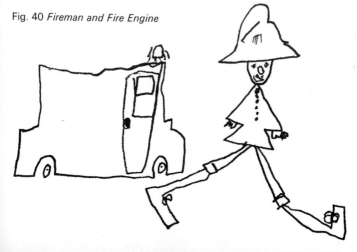

Fig. 41 A Fireman one year later has become simpler and less energetic

Fig. 42

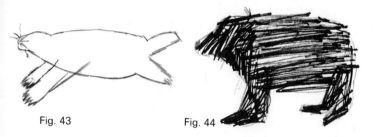

Fig. 43   Fig. 44

the aeroplane-conscious child to the airport, the animal-lover to the zoo. Suggest to the would-be aviator that he draw a picture of 'I am getting into the plane' or to the animal-lover 'I am looking at a giraffe'. The point there is one of identification of the child with a subject he already feels drawn towards. Suggestions for help should make him conscious of himself and his body. The fireman drawing (fig. 40) was observed acutely as a result of identification by the boy with his subjects. So, one does not say vaguely 'why not paint a farm'? but specifically, 'paint the time when we went to visit the farm'; not, 'paint a holiday picture', so much as something specific like 'paint, we go to the sea and I dig trenches in the sand'. The more emotionally interested and involved the child is in any subject, the more meaningful to him the work he does as a result.

There are of course differences in the interests of girls and boys, so that while girls like their home and pets, boys may be picturing themselves on tractors and drawing roadworks and mechanical diggers.

Through the six to nine period the child lives out an attitude to colour which is purely emotional. And to insist on a child painting his grass green or his roofs red would be to push him towards something he is perhaps not emotionally ready for. Grass is not always green. In a hot summer, parts of it may be brown. If someone has used weed-killer the grass may be patchy. Anyone attempting to encourage the child to an untrue supposition that grass should always be painted green might certainly be glossing over something the child should be able to question and observe for himself.

The child must observe for himself. When he queries colour— 'what colour is the sky'?—one might ask 'what sky'? The sky today, which is full of scudding grey clouds, and sometimes

Fig. 45 Careful observation and thought about the character of a tree's growth produced this majestic picture

Fig. 46 *Trees and birds and me*

Fig. 47 *Landscape with Road*

patches of blue, but everywhere peach coloured reflections of sunlight on cloud? Or do you mean yesterday's sky? then it was all blue, pale near the horizon and darker and richer above. Let him go out and look, for the fact that he has asked presupposes the energy to sustain him through to the answer.

'Playing' with natural materials is something that is enjoyed by the pre-tens. The pastime becomes more sophisticated as the child grows older. This younger stage of making things which can be exploited in play situations is a rewarding one for the parent. The toy cart which has lost its rear wheels was upturned and ready to be thrown away. Only a very trained eye for the unusual or the child's wondering pleasure in the bizarre could have made it metamorphose so simply (fig. 49).

The stone squirrel in the picture came from a collection of odd stones and with plasticine and drinking straw it looks just like a squirrel eating a nut. Links with the child's experience are always there somewhere.

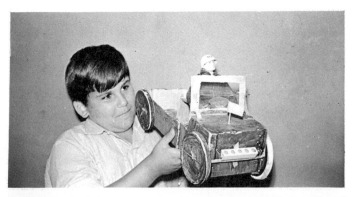

Fig. 48 The child above was given a set of tools: simple but good, well proportioned ones. He was shown how to use them, given some off-cuts of board, a bundle of laths and some nails, and left on his own. When children know how to cut straight and know how to hit a nail properly, with a minimum of good tools they will do no serious damage to themselves.

Fig. 49 Picture of a toy lorry which became a toad

Fig. 50 A squirrel

Fig. 51 Carving from a block of household salt. See under 'Carving'

Adding a dimension

All children particularly towards nine years old, derive great pleasure from the realism they can achieve with clay. Children often model clay figures to use as puppets. They stand them up, sit them down, shake them by the hand and talk for them. Modelling in clay consisting of pulling and twisting the material is not technically demanding, and this is the use to which it is put by the eight year-old. Technically clay is an 'adding to' medium, while carving—of wood, clay, soap, block salt or plaster—is one of taking away. The pre-tens observe few of the niceties, preferring to combine techniques to get the result. Carving or whittling, if you introduce them in the home, are better done by one child at a time on his own, than by a small group, who might get too excited. It is important to teach a child to hold a knife properly, cutting away from himself, with the non-cutting hand protected; knives are fascinating and super-vision may be found necessary.

The parent will need to be around when the children are printing, too. Prints can be made from natural objects stuck on a block, from cardboard, from mosaics—anything at all with a raised surface. Linoleum and wood blocks, of course, need gouging out with the correct tools, and here the proper way to hold the tool to avoid accidents is the first thing one teaches. You can see from the picture (fig. 52) that the non-cutting hand is holding the block firmly, behind the movement of the cutting edge.

The same materials and techniques apply to children of this age level as to those of pre-school age (see page 28). Also recommended are needlework collage (page 85), fabric dyeing (page 102), papier mâché (page 90), potato and cardboard printing (page 66), balsa constructions and advanced puppet making (pages 62 and 77).

Fig. 52 The correct way to make a lino-cut avoiding risk of accident

Fig. 53

5 Nine to twelve plus

The nines and tens have usually established a break away from their younger brothers and sisters. To begin with they are now definitely boys and girls, and they see and depict people, as being one or the other. Dress consciousness comes with the awareness of sex differences, and clothes are indicated and often shown in detail in their pictures.

Girls are now interested in drawing and designing clothes, they like ganging up and sitting together, going to a film show together, establishing close relationships with several other girls at a time. In their drawings ten year-olds search for the right face colour; hair is carefully styled and each of the features in the face is detailed and easily recognisable. Consider the facial features in any of the illustrations for the six to nine year-old stage (fig. 53). Isolate them from their position on the face and their identity is lost. Puff sleeves, panels in a dress, buckles, cuffs are all noted by the ten year-old girl.

The kind of observation a girl gives to clothes, houses, flowers and animals, a boy gives to his ships and aeroplanes. He brings to bear a new analytical approach and a detailed and accurate way of working. The boy tends not to be as lyrical as

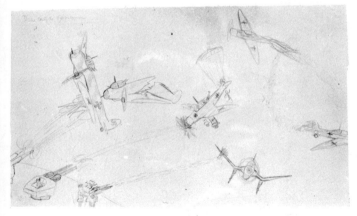

Fig. 54 *Air Battle.* This child pours out battle pictures, but researches carefully to get models, uniforms, and equipment correct in minutest detail.

the girl, but seems to concentrate on visual relationships of detail and perspective. Because they are striving for something which is difficult to attain—a more adult standard of realism—the temptation to give up the effort seems to be very strong.

The fact that the child is also discontented with his output makes the situation no easier.

Children of this age group can long to paint like the smart advertisements, and given a repertoire of slick techniques finds that there is progress towards that ambition. Success makes him or her stay in that groove for a long time, smothered with praise from other children and teacher, and with mother probably thinking her child is showing talent at last.

The long-haired full-busted lovely in the picture illustrated was presumably drawn in this manner (one of many on sketch-pads), because the small underdeveloped artist wished she could grow a bit. The rest of the picture—*A Windy Day*—has not been thought about, and means almost nothing, because the child's thought was so concentrated on her problem.

Fig. 55

A group of these small girls, eleven and twelve year-olds, moaned all through an art period in school. Their drawing was 'terrible' and would I come and 'give them a start'. They actually wanted part of the picture painted for them . . . We questioned around the group, found that they had never actually looked closely at a figure to find out how it worked, and finally they sat down to a bit of hard observation. They produced drawings of the quality of the one shown (fig. 55) which is very like the sitter indeed. They approached the figure from the mechanical point of view as well as trying to get an accurate likeness. The child shown would have difficulty standing up as her legs would not hinge from the hips, but that distortion is as nothing compared with the fight and achievement.

Fig. 56

The picture in figure 56 was drawn by a child who was deaf. Notice his preoccupation with the ears, whose lack of function in himself had drawn his attention to their importance in others. The child who is laughed at may always have one lone person in his pictures standing apart from the group. The delicate boy may only care to draw muscle men.

A little nine year-old girl, who desperately wanted a baby sister or brother, for months made drawings only of babies in prams and carriages. The drawing (fig. 57a) shows that she is still in the schematic stage, as the figure is static and features out of their context would be unrecognisable. The only thing which might indicate her age is the overlap of pram on top of the figure —

Fig. 57 a and b

the shoes come out again under the pram. This overlapping is typical of the nines to twelves. Her great need may well have blocked her development for a time. When her mother was eight months pregnant the girl crayoned the picture (fig. 57b) of the baby in its pram outside the child's house. That was the last pram she drew, because she knew she was going to get what she wanted.

Co-operation with others

This is a good time for group work, when children will embark on big pictorial products. Some of them are more self-critical than others, and find it impossible to do what they want to do artistically. These children mix well in group activities with the others.

The cardboard container in which a new ice-box was delivered provided a marvellous outlet for a group of small boys, who begged all kinds and colours of paint from their parents, and gave it the now fashionable 'psychedelic' decoration, to help along their feeling of a 'Time Machine' journeying through space backwards and forwards through time. It was great fun as a group project, and, with its door cut into the front can be played with by the gang. With the door cut in two horizontally like a stable door it also has possibilities as a puppet theatre, or a Punch and Judy show. The cost of having to house it will never equal its value to the boys.

Fig. 58 *The Time Machine*

Any project can be carried out together, such as a group model of a camp, or a real island which the children know about, or a model of their part of a town, or perhaps of a fair that has just arrived. These ideas need paper, papier mâché (wet newspaper kneaded to a workable dough), an old table, and lots of poster or powder paint. Perhaps a mosaic technique might be incorporated, and all sorts of textures embedded in a solid base for the project. Shoe boxes and cardboard of all kinds also scraps of fabric could be used for models, especially of the fairground. Boys of ten or so are usually mechanically minded or have a certain knowledge of how to make a model work.

Boys will dig out complicated trench hide-outs in the garden, and emerge at a signal with flags flying to fight the girls. Girls quite often lead wars against the boys, but, taking advantage of the different rate of learning which exists between boys and girls, they sometimes carry out their warfare on a verbal level, involving question and answer on matters of fact, in which the girls often stand to win. The gangs have shared interests, probably each has a code and a special language, and the group is a way of sinking personal differences and deficiencies below noticing level. The group is more powerful than one person, and where a child is naturally restrained he may feel the confidence to grow more courageous under this new umbrella. An independence of the adult opinion seems to characterise this age, but it is modified by the child's lack of experience.

Anyone who is unaware that the group stage is important, and who tries to prolong the period of dependence on the adult could be inviting trouble. Trying to break up this new interdependence of children in their gang has been known to drive them to secrecy and make them much less co-operative all round.

There is a saying in schools that 'one should ask, not tell'. There are ways of asking, of course, other than saying 'would you mind doing . . .' A most efficient method if a group of children need assistance or need employment, is to say 'Will you help me to . . .' do whatever you feel *they* most want to do. That could be anything, from finding out about the exact uniforms of the armies fighting at Culloden, or the American Civil War, to assembling materials for a mural to fit the hall wall—and actually hanging it there afterwards for an acceptable period. One has to be fairly generous with one's time if one wants to give one's child a balanced development in the creative sense. Keep in mind on the child's need to be given responsibility and give it to

Figs. 59 and 60 Of the sixty feet long mural shown here, and in colour on page 54, sections were allotted to single children or to groups. The general theme of 'How Things Began' unites the different styles.

those who are a nuisance. Put them in charge of the paints, for example, when the garage, terrace, or flat roof has been transformed to a mural-painting factory. From the early primary school stage they should have found that work is fun, and that to get most satisfaction one has to apply oneself with concentration.

The mural in the illustration (fig. 59) is, when complete, sixty feet long, and is the combined work of groups of boys and girls with the same idea. The theme is 'How things began', and, with each child having an area to himself or herself, there are several points of view on the subject. A mural is, strictly speaking, a decoration applied directly to the wall. At home, however, large areas of wall space being limited, it is practical to consider putting a decoration onto a surface to be pinned to the wall when it is finished. Large sheets of thick brown paper will do; two or three sheets glued or taped together at the edge would allow several children to work at a time.

Anything large would be a good beginning. An old curtain could give scope for improvisation, as it would take all kinds of different materials, applied in various ways. Buttons could be sewn to it, embroidery to attach rope, straws or fabric could be sewn with a bodkin (a blunt needle) and string, leaves and seeds, photographs from magazines, and fabric scraps could all be glued to it. Use a strong vegetable glue, or a rubber based one, for good results. Murals are decorations, differing from paintings, which can become too narrow a view.

Perhaps a curtain, such as the one discussed, with a decorative pattern all over it, could be used to screen a show of the group's own puppets. Puppets can be the beginning of a great deal of play, and sometimes draw out previously hidden dramatic talent as well. The materials they can be made in depend a little on the amount of supervision the children are to have. A very effective little hand puppet can be made from a deep paper bag. The face can be the bottom of the bag, and is painted. Hair, or other additions—big nose, ears, side-whiskers—can be glued on. Tie the bag at the neck and make small armoles at the two sides. With the hand and forearm inside the bag, the thumb and little finger act as puppet arms through the armholes, and three middle fingers go through the tied neck into the head. A nice touch is the addition of clothing with sleeves to cover the thumb and little finger.

A puppet with a papier mâché head takes a little longer to achieve, but is very rewarding to make. Once the pulp of soaked

Fig. 63 Paper bag puppet or mask. See also under 'Puppets'

newspaper and water is kneaded to a good modelling consistency the head can be started. Roll a pellet of plasticine to the size and length of three fingers tightly together. The papier mâché is modelled on top of it in any shape for a puppet head; it would be a human or an animal. Leave the head to dry overnight with a coating of glue all over it. When dry, the plasticine can be gently removed, the little bits adhering taken out with a teaspoon. The head can be painted and left to dry hung over a piece of stick standing in a cotton reel (spool). All that remains is for clothing to be made; a simple nightgown shape with small sleeves to cover little finger and thumb. To make each of the puppets have a different character, their clothes could be decorated, with potato prints, or dyed bright clear colours and trimmed with colourful ribbon. Hair, stuck on to the head, could be wool, yarn, a string duster, or perhaps drinking straws. Opportunities for invention are endless.

Fig. 64 Hand puppet, which is animated by the middle three fingers into the hollow head, and thumb and little finger in each of the sleeves.

Shaping standards

One cannot overemphasise the value of the child's making things like this for himself, using easily obtainable materials which he himself has found, rather than kits of pre-cut shapes which are bought and put together, ending their short lives as dangerous pieces of plastic, shattered in a toy-box. Packaged sets for the young weaver, for sewing, jewelry making and making model aeroplanes, etc., fall into this category. The pre-cut sections are often tiny, ill-fitting, and generally unsatisfactory in that they fall to pieces often before they are completed. Children get great satisfaction from improvising.

Give the child the opportunity to see good examples of whatever he is most interested in. Trips to museums, to craftsmen, and to public gardens where unusual plants are grown can be a great stimulus to a child when they relate to what he is doing. If he

Fig. 65

plans to make a coiled pot, the local museum will have examples from all over the world. Printed and woven designs of fabric can be seen not only in museums, but in good department stores, where a child can see how a design folds and drapes. The potential sculptor, cutting shapes from salt, soap or wax, or making clay models, might benefit from a visit to the zoo or local pet shop to sort out any particular difficulties. The nine year-old's drawing (fig. 68) was the result of finding a very interesting plant he had never seen before in a part of the country he was visiting. He later found it was a weed, but was still just as intrigued.

It is important for children to see things of a high standard of design which other people have made. They also need to have from their parents the assurance that they too are capable of worthwhile effort. Children respond to a challenging situation. It gives them interest and a sense of purpose, and above all confidence and a feeling of mastery. For adults to put a use to their dyed or potato-printed fabric, by making it up into a curtain, or garment is the most effective sort of encouragement.

Fig. 66 A two colour fabric design made by lino printing; this is the work of a pre-school child. Notice snow dropping from the sky line.

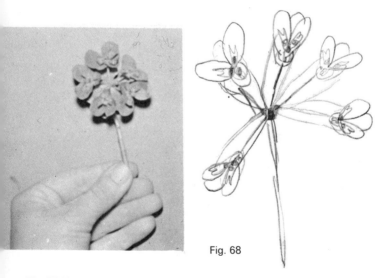

Fig. 68

Fig. 67 The small plant from which the drawing (fig. 68) was made

Fig. 69 *Walking in Space*

Better still, children might make their own clothes, curtains and drapes for their rooms, with their designs in block printing, batik, and tie-and-dye. Given challenges like these the child will find it easier to take on more difficult problems, so that uncertainties may give place entirely to self-confidence and a pride in his work. It is important at this period in his school life when the child is so very self-critical and uncertain, that one should not demand more than he is capable of, so running the risk that he never finishes anything.

As a guide to evaluation of home projects one might suggest that you consider the following:

Whether the child chose the project himself.

Did he manage the tools reasonably well?

Is he using the correct materials—ought drawing and painting materials to be checked to see that they are fine/large enough?

Has he worked within his own ability, or is he assuming or striving towards adult values?

Have his painting and drawing developed unevenly, with some things understood, and some things left in an immature style?

Has he been unduly influenced by adult taste or his need for adult or parental approval?

Is he pleased with what he has done, and has the family shown their appreciation?

60

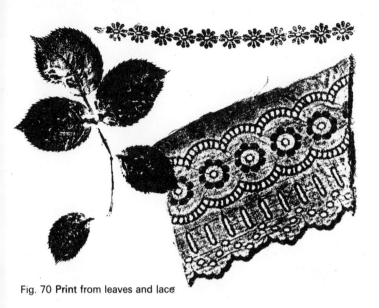

Fig. 70 **Print** from leaves and lace

Has it been fun; was it spontaneous and zestful?

As the child grows older, what he actually makes in his creative periods has more and more significance for him. Earlier his output was prodigious; now, work takes longer to achieve, and to maintain the original spark of invention through to the final product is more difficult. The adult parent has also to ask how to prepare the child. How to encourage him to be proud of what he makes and does, instead of dissatisfied with it. What he produces in terms of art should be seen, by the adult, as an indication of direction. Not necessarily saying 'he's always going to think that way' but, 'tomorrow may be different'.

Children from nine to twelve work in groups on murals and mosaics (see pages 81 and 83). They continue modelling in clay and plasticine and with wire constructions (pages 81 and 95), printing from lino cuts or wood (page 80). Also recommended are brass and candle rubbings (page 65), wax crayon, scraper-board (page 103) and carving in salt, plaster or stone (page 67).

Glossary of techniques

Abstract Painting

Abstract painting involves arriving at the essence of the subject by use of simplified shapes. Abstractions are not always achieved by geometrical shapes, just simplified ones, like the example below (fig. 72). A whole abstract picture of construction can be made with one kind of material, whether it is tissue paper, powder paint or poster colour, balsa wood or milk bottle tops. Different colours can be used, with large simple areas next to each other. The problem lies in the correct balance of values between the areas.

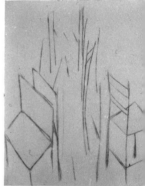

Fig. 71 A straightforward drawing of a group of chairs

Fig. 72 An abstraction of the same group of chairs, the same basic lines, but a simplification.

Balsa Wood

Balsa, a very light wood, can be bought from shops which stock models and construction kits. It can be easily cut with a tool (Stanley knife or a Swann-Morton tool) and it comes in convenient lengths and sheets of different sizes.

The model shop will also sell the appropriate glue in different quantities. Obviously a large size will be more economical, but unless the stopper is replaced at once after use, the balsa cement hardens and much will be wasted.

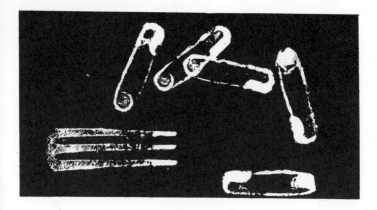

Fig. 73 The high dive of a safety pin. An impress on balsa wood. See also under 'Balsa': but a similar print could be made by pressing objects into a piece of polystyrene.

Construction of all kinds can be made in balsa, as the cement dries so quickly that almost as the next length is cut the previous piece of wood will be secure.

Prints can be made from balsa, because it is so soft that anything hard pressed into it leaves an imprint which can be clearly seen when the surface is inked. Follow the printing technique describing linoleum printing, obviously using a wide piece of balsa fixed into place on a block of some kind. Ink it and put the paper over it to receive the print.

Bamboo Pens

Bamboo pens can be made and used for drawing simply by cutting the end with a sharp knife. Take a length of bamboo cane, either the kind from the garden, or that can be bought

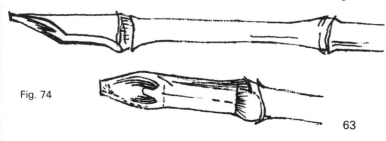

Fig. 74

from a garden store, provided it has a **softish core**. **W**ith a sharp knife cut the end in a curve (fig. 74) making a nib. Cut a final snick up the nib for a quarter of an inch to allow a little movement of the nib, otherwise the line made by the pen will be too hard.

Batik Printing

Batik is a fabric printing technique which originated in Java, and works on the principle that dried wax will not absorb a fabric dye. Older children enjoy it very much.

Beeswax and candle wax are melted in a double boiler saucepan or pot. When hot, it is painted on to stretched-out material, in any design of the child's choice. It could be a flower pattern, an abstract composition of lines, or linear drawing.

The fabric should be fairly thin for good results. Too heavy a material sometimes has to be waxed on both sides, which can make the job tedious for a child.

When the wax has cooled and hardened, dip the material into a cold water dye, squeeze and hang up to dry. The wax will chip off like candle drips, but it can also be difficult to remove. Never attempt the removal over a sink without a strainer. Try to chip off as much as possible, but ironing between blotting paper can be effective, renewing the blotting paper each time the wax soaks it (newspaper can be used instead of blotting paper).

Another method of removing the wax is to boil the dyed fabric in water with washing soda. Rinse in a bowl of cold water and the wax should rise to the top.

Brushes

Until children are capable of making an evaluation of brushes in relation to what they can achieve with them, you must be the provider of general all-purpose brushes which will last as long as possible. For this, the medium-sized hog hair bristle brushes are best with powder paints or poster colour and cold water glues.

If possible children should have a range of brushes which should include small soft ones, a small hog hair bristle with a round end, and a few medium with flat and rounded ends. 'A workman cannot be better than his tools' certainly applies to brushes. Get them from a good artists' shop and you will find that the length of use and wear you get will be cheap at the price.

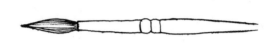

Fig. 75 Left. Flat hog hair brush
Above. Medium rounded hog hair brush
Below. Soft squirrel-hair brush

They should of course—need it be said—be washed carefully and thoroughly after each use, and stored upright in a jar, brush end uppermost. Periodically it is worthwhile giving the brushes an additional wash in soapy water as a conditioner. They should then be tied together and hung up to drip dry, and stored as before.

Brushes should never be left standing in paint water, even for a short time, as this will spoil their shape.

Candle Rubbings and Drawing

For this you need a stump of candle, any thick paper—cartridge, sugar or construction paper, brown wrapping paper—brush and powder or poster colour, or ebony stain, or shoe polish; a knife for trimming a drawing point on the candle.

First a drawing is made on the paper with the candle, making sure that the wax candle makes quite a thick line. The colour can then be painted flowingly over the paper, and will roll off the surface of the wax, leaving the candle lines white and giving the effect of a print.

The candle drawings shown (fig. 76) are free-hand, straight on to the paper, and are of the pattern made by half a cut lemon. Some kitchen paper towel was dipped in shoe polish and smoothed over the surface. Because the paper was smooth surfaced the polish rubbed off a little to give a grey effect.

Fig. 76

Rubbings of all sorts of textural surfaces can be made: brick, wood grain, perforated zinc, tree bark, rippled glass. This may need two children working together, one holding the paper still, the other to do the rubbing. Lay the paper firmly on the object and rub over the whole area of the paper with the candle. Make sure that the paper is pressed down on the texture enough for a good all over rubbing. If a bark rubbing is being done make sure that the paper is large enough to show the growth well. Work over the finished rubbings with brush strokes of the stain or paint.

Cardboard Printing

Cardboard cuts are inexpensive and very simple to make.

Two pieces of carboard of the same size are needed, with newsprint for printing on; a flat baking tin and rubber roller, and water bound printing ink.

As children can't easily cut intricate shapes from cardboard they have to work in uncomplicated blocks. Designs are cut from the second piece of cardboard and the shapes which result from free cutting are stuck on to the other piece of cardboard. There should be only small spaces between the cardboard shapes set

Fig. 77 Print made from cut pieces of cornflake packet

on their background card, as the inking roller might otherwise smudge ink into them and spoil the print.

Large swirling shapes, rather than anything figurative, are most successful. Ink is squeezed out on to the baking tin and the roller moved up and down until covered with a thin layer of ink. Move the roller briskly over the mounted card to be printed until the ink sticks onto the surface. Put the inked card on to a clean sheet of newspaper so that any smudges are not transferred to the print; put a piece of paper on top and rub all over with a spoon, so that the ink underneath sticks to the paper and makes a print.

Carving

Children find carving very satisfying as it involves working all round something. Unusual materials for carving are plaster blocks, bars of salt and bars of soap. Each has its own qualities: one hard, the others soft. Children discover their own preferences, finding that what they can achieve depends upon the character of the material.

Shapes in salt or soap should be kept as simple as possible, whereas plaster enables one to cut a little detail as it is a harder substance.

Many other materials can of course be used. Found objects, chalk picked up on the beach, drift-wood or old wooden blocks can be worked on with the simplest tools. A small claw chisel or a plain cold steel chisel from a hardware store can be used for

Fig. 78

chipping stone or brick, tapped with a mallet or hammer. But for softer materials such as chalk, plaster, soap or salt a sharp penknife or tool and a selection of sandpaper are all that is needed. The salt carving shown (fig. 78) was made with a kitchen knife.

Whatever is being carved, have it done outside where the bits can be swept up, or spread newspaper widely indoors. There always seem to be more shavings than masterpieces.

Charcoal

This material can be bought in sticks which are potentially very messy and are extremely brittle. Once these characteristics are realised a child can work to great effect with this dense black drawing material, getting subtle greys to velvet darks, light thin lines and thick wide ones, depending entirely on how it is used. I would recommend holding the charcoal stick in tissue paper.

Charcoal drawings need fixing with a shellac spray or fixative otherwise they easily smudge.

Collage

Collage is a French word meaning glueing or pasting, and as an art term refers to sticking down or putting together in a picture all sorts of collected things like old photographs, postage stamps, bus tickets, pictures from magazines and so on. The emphasis in this medium is on the interest of the objects put together, so apart from a stiffish surface on which to work—cardboard, hardboard or heavy wrapping paper—glue is virtually the only expense involved.

Children may derive pleasure from looking for and gathering together objects for collage, but sometimes need help in the actual job of assembly. If they have a lot of things to stick, the task may look formidable. On the whole the most successful collages are basically simple ones, containing not too many different kinds of objects. Too wide a range of objects, for instance, scrap metal, cotton reels (spools), paper junk, involves problems of sticking as well as arrangement.

There is no need for collages to be representational in intent; the technique is rather one of matching objects, colours or textures. A good glue is essential, and will vary with objects to be stuck. An impact glue or contact cement must be used for metals. White glue could be used for papers, and a transparent rubber-based adhesive works well on most fabrics.

Crayon

Soft wax crayons, thick enough to hold in the hand comfortably, are the small child's first drawing material. A good dense line can be made with them, and areas of intense colour can be filled in with a side-to-side movement. With large wax crayons a child can successfully 'paint' a big picture, about fifteen inches by twenty, on smooth, non-absorbent paper.

There are slimmer wax crayons available, and often the colours are not dense and the crayon slides across the paper not making much of a line. These are to be avoided in favour of a softer variety. It should not be necessary to fix a crayon drawing with fixative.

Pencil crayons, or coloured pencils are suitable for drawing on a small scale. Used occasionally they are fine as a drawing technique, but used always because they are colourful and less trouble to provide and prepare than paints and brushes, they are a poor **substitute**.

Fig. 79a *In the Garden* by a six year-old boy. Notice the perspective introduced into the shed sides. Awareness of this illusion is not to be forced, as it comes as a result of the child's own work, in his time rather than yours. Fig. 79b *Cowboy*, a crayon drawing.

70

James

Fig. 81 *Man in the Moon* brush drawing by a nursery school child

Fig. 82 *Army Charge* pencil drawing by a seven year old

Drawing

Drawing, as a co-ordination of arm, hand and medium resulting in line, is the first two-dimensional art form a child knows. The young child uses a broad free approach, so needs similar qualities of materials. Large drawing sticks (fig. 21), giant wax crayons and large soft pencils should be provided for use on large sheets of paper, say fifteen by twenty inches. Directions for making marker sticks from bamboo cane are given on page 21.

On the whole, pencil drawing is for the older child who has the muscular control to handle the finer character of the medium.

Drawings should be considered an end in themselves, not as a preliminary to colouring or painting.

Dyeing

Cold water dyes are most convenient for use at home, although there are other, more involved and more expensive systems.

It is possible to dye fabrics simply and easily with potassium permanganate, which can be bought in very small quantities from most chemists and drug stores. Pour about two pints of scalding water into a bowl or pail containing a tablespoonful of the potassium. Stir to help it dissolve. The fabric can be dipped into it, moved around with the spoon to let the dye cover it, taken out, and rinsed and dried. If the material looks only pale brown after the first dip, keep on dipping and drying until the required depth of tint is reached, as more chemical added to the amount of water will rot the fabric.

Dyeing is a pleasant activity in itself, but it can be a starter for other techniques, such as fabric printing with linoleum or potato, batik printing, tie-dyeing and discharge patterning with lemon juice. (See below.)

Discharge Printing

A plastic squeezer of lemon juice can be used to draw a random pattern on a stretched piece of material dyed with potassium permanganate. The lemon will drain the area it touches of its colour, leaving it anything from palest yellow to white. A cut potato dipped into a saucer of lemon juice, used as printing ink, or a cut stick can be very effective as pattern makers.

Engraving

Engraving is a process of scratching a linear drawing onto a flat surface as a preliminary to printing. Most usually one would use plaster, wood or wax.

For plaster engraving (a simple technique for a child), a rectangular block is made as described under Plaster Carving (page 94), only it should be flat. Lines can easily be cut with a nail or other sharp point, into the surface of the plaster, to be printed with water-bound printing ink. The drawn line must be a sixteenth of an inch deep, otherwise the printing ink will blot into the line and obscure the drawing. The surface is inked with a roller and the incised lines will print white.

Wood engraving and wax engraving are described on page 103.

Fig. 83 Engraving on a plaster tile. See also page 93

Exhibitions

As much as possible of children's work ought to be displayed in

the home, and not entirely in their own rooms. Children greatly value the 'vote of confidence' shown by exhibiting their work prominently in the living area of the home. As children quickly lose a sense of involvement in their own work, displays should change regularly and often. A convenient method of display, because it takes drawing pins (thumbtacks), is insulation board or fibre board, which can be bought in sizes to measure, and is simple to fix. Pictures can be pinned straight on to the board.

Otherwise a small collection of frames could be made, of the size a child works to, so that frequent interchange of pictures is possible. Pictures in frames look better mounted on cardboard, or behind a window mount. If the card is white it is suitable for all kinds of pictures. (See Mounting Pictures, page 83.)

Fabric Painting

If fabric is stretched on a board it can be painted with cold water dye. Interesting effects can be reached by first drawing on the fabric with a candle, then painting over this with two or three dye colours. When the dyes are dry the candle can be ironed off between sheets of blotting paper as described for Batik.

Fabric Printing

The glaze (size or filler) in new material has to be washed out, before printing ink or dye will adhere. The material should be stretched and smoothed and placed on newspaper. Then any flat surface (linoleum, potato, plaster) cut and prepared with a design for printing can be inked and placed at intervals on the fabric. A regular pattern means placing the motifs close together.

Stencils can be used for printing fabric. These are cards with shapes cut out of them; stencils are laid on the fabric and ink has to be sprayed on. As sprays for this purpose may not be commonly found in the home, a teastrainer and an old toothbrush will do, the brush being dipped into fairly wet printing ink and rubbed round the inside of the strainer, which is held above the stencil.

Fabric printing can be done with cold water dyes or printing inks. The inks are obtainable either water-based or oily, but the water ones wash out in a short time, although they are easier to clean up. The oil-based inks have to be cleaned off with turpentine or white spirit, but are fairly permanent on the fabric.

Figs. 84 and 85 The sliced potato, the cut surface, and the print. This simple process makes potato printing ideal for printing on fabric.

Finger Painting

For this one needs fairly thick cold water paste, a large brush or piece of sponge, powder colours, yoghourt containers, large sheets of wrapping paper of other non-absorbent surfaced paper and several pieces of cardboard.

Put newspaper down first to protect the table or floor. Make up the powder colours in their containers. Spread the paste onto the thick paper, and colour with the dilute powder paints. The fingers mix the colours into the paste, but all kinds of utensils can be used as well as fingers and thumbs to create lines, shapes and textures, such as the serrated edge of a piece of cardboard, knitting needles or a lightly held fork.

A small child may like to make a blot picture, which entails the spreading of plain paste on to a surface and distributing paint or ink on the right or left half of the sheet. The paper is folded over in the centre and the two sides are brought together and 'blotted' while the surface is still wet. A blot picture can be made by putting a dry second paper onto the first piece which has been spread and coloured, then peeling the two sheets apart very quickly (before drying), leaving a pulled-up texture.

Folding Over Painting

This technique is effective—and quick—using thick paint or printing ink. First paint one side of the paper, then fold the paper sides together and blot. Effects are fortuitous, but good fun.

Fixative is necessary on pastel, charcoal and soft pencil drawings to avoid smudges. It sells in small bottles with sprays operated by blowing, but is also available in convenient spray-can aerosol packs.

Fig. 86

Fig. 87

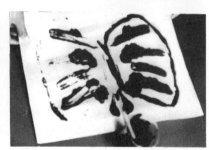

Fig. 88

Glove Puppets

Glove puppet is a generic term used to describe a doll whose actions are controlled by a hand inside, and need not necessarily be made with a glove.

A head can be made of papier mâché as described later. The decoration of the head and the dressing of the doll should be designed to bring out the character of the doll. Hair, stuck-on absorbent cotton or wool in strands, can be thick or thin and

Fig. 89 This puppet is a gentle, beautiful one, from its rough wool hair to its dress. The necklace is of painted dried melon seeds. A tougher character of puppet should be made with exaggerated features, so that its identity is easy to distinguish.

straggly. Grotesque noses, big ears, blackened teeth, are part of the heightened emotion of puppetry. The width of dress from sleeve to cuff should be only a little more than the width of the child operator's outstretched hand, and the dress should be cut simply. The neck of the dress fits over the ridge made on the base of the head.

When the hand goes in to work the puppet, the little finger and thumb go into each of the sleeves, and the three fingers left fit into the tube cavity inside the head.

Glue

For glue, see under Collage.

Linear Pattern

This drawing began as a kind of doodle, but ended up as a

Fig. 90 An all-over linear pattern using the human figure as a basis

careful study of figures. The original idea was that all the space left around a first figure should be filled by some part of subsequent figures.

Lino Cutting

Linoleum for cutting can be bought from artists' shops, but can be readily obtained elsewhere. It must be plain: cork or fairly thick composition, not inlaid or plastic.

Lino cutting tools can often be bought at a stationer's, if not at the art shop. You need one handle, and two or three nibs, one a little V-shape, another perhaps broader, and a gouge for removing a lot at a time.

Many children like to cut straight into the lino, knowing where to cut, but some prefer first to draw or trace their design on to the lino. Linoleum will crack when one attempts to cut fine detail; it is essentially a medium for simplicity, so large forms should be kept to. The V-shaped tools are used to cut a line out or to cut closely along a raised line. For a lino-line to print black, the space around it has to be cut away. If a line is cut away while the rest of the lino surface stays, the line is not inked and prints as white on black.

For lino-printing see Printing.

Masks

Paper plates, scissors, a stapler or glue, and paint for decorating are all that are needed for one kind of mask-making, although masks can be made from papier-mâché, paper bags or cardboard boxes.

Fig. 91 Plasticine head by a ten year-old girl

Using the paper plate method, the holes for eyes and nose can be cut out, and eyebrow and nose shapes built up in papier-mâché. But whether shapes are modelled and stuck on or just painted, the ears, hair, moustaches, beards, hats, crown and so on can be added. Elastic or tapes attached from holes just above the ears will keep the mask onto the child's head. See Paper Masks.

Modelling

Clay and plasticine are the two materials most used for modelling. Plasticine, although it can get hard, does not dry out, and can be used endlessly. It is, however, more expensive than clay, which can be bought ready made up in plastic bags, or in powder form to be mixed at home.

Clay dries quickly and has to be kept damp with wet rags, or put back into its pail with a lid or topping of wet rags. Once a model or pot has dried it cannot be added to, as wet clay does not stick to dry; the only thing to do with the model is to wet it and start again.

Children need few tools, but iced lolly sticks can be useful. When a child makes a model he may want to fire it in a kiln for permanence; if you have access to a kiln, the model should dry out for about two weeks before firing. Baking in a hot oven cannot guarantee permanence; if the clay shapes being baked are heavy and thick they will probably break, and the oven is only hot enough really to dry the model through.

For modelling in clay, a large drawing board is ideal to work on. Failing that a large sheet of greaseproof (waxed or plastic) paper taped down on to a tray is very effective.

A modelling dough can be made by putting a cup of salt into a cup of water. Stir over heat. Take off the heat and add a cup of flour creamed in half a cup of water. Mix together quickly, not letting it get lumpy. It should be a heavy dough, but if it remains soft, heat gently, stirring till it thickens. The mixture can be coloured with food colourants, but will keep indefinitely if kept moist in a plastic bag. Models, if left to dry, can then be painted

Mosaics

Mosaics can be made from pebbles, broken china pieces, set into a cement base of some kind with little spaces left around

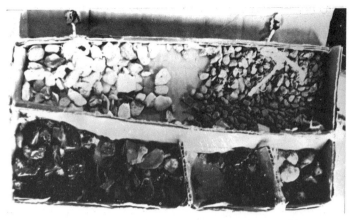

Fig. 92 (a) Homemade box made by an eight year-old for his collection
of coloured stones
(b) Mosaic made from the same collection of stones

each piece. The pleasure of mosaic lies in the correct matching of
the colours and textures of the materials, so it can be achieved by
using cut-out or torn coloured papers or photographs equally as
well as with harder materials.

82

For paper mosaics good effects can be got by using a dark paper as base.

When collecting stones or pebbles for mosaic only smooth ones should be chosen, although any shape can be used. For the mosaic shown (fig. 92b) the pebbles were picked up on the bank of a river, and were black, cream, red, brown and green. They were set into plaster of Paris, on greaseproof (waxed) paper with a plasticine surround. Mosaic materials can also be stuck to hardboard with white glue.

Mounting Pictures

If frames are used for displaying pictures, mounts (mats) placed inside the frames set off the pictures well.

A window mount (mat) can be cut from a piece of white, cream or grey cardboard measured to fit inside the frame. With a lightly pencilled guide-line cut out a rectangle (with a cutting tool), slightly smaller than the picture to be displayed. The window should be cut with the two sides the same distance from the edges of the card, but with slightly more cardboard at the bottom than at the top.

If you are going to display using only a mount (mat), put a back on it and stick a plastic sheet over the front. Thread a thin cord or wire through the backing by which to hang it.

Murals

The making of murals, pictures to decorate a wall, usually involves group work. Small children do not find it easy to work together without an adult working closely with them. Interesting wall pictures can be made, though, from cut-outs from several pictures of similar subjects all stuck onto a large 'back-cloth'. Many composite pictures by nursery school children achieved in this way are exhibited every year.

Murals more true to the meaning of the term can be painted direct onto paper or wall by a group of children each having an area to cover. The pictures (fig. 59) show parts of a mural sixty feet long, painted in a school corridor by a class of ten and eleven year-olds. They used whatever paint they could get and house painters' brushes.

Fig. 93 Another view of the mural painted along a primary school corridor

Needlework

Needlework is basically the use of needle and thread, and is not just for girls. Pictures can be made with needles and wool, string, heavy cotton and thread used to bind objects on to a hessian (burlap) backing. Needlework is not only embroidery, and, using large needles and heavy threads some valuable picture-making can be done with a minimum of pretty stitches and a maximum of sewn-on textures.

Interesting pictures in line can be made with a binding stitch, holding down string laid in lines to suggest recognisable shapes.

Painting

There are several different kinds of material with which to paint, varying in suitability for different age groups of children.

'Gouache' is basically a water-colour medium, with the use of opaque white to mix with and thicken some of the colours.

Powder colour is a medium which allows colour to be mixed and put on thickly with large brushes. It is particularly recommended for small children. The powder can be bought in tins from which the colour can be spooned into individual containers, preferably with lids. It is then mixed with water to the consistency of thick soup (like poster colour), and a brush kept aside for each container of colour. If a group of children are working together it is not always essential for each child to have his own set of colours, as long as there is a central 'bank' of pots from which he can choose. The younger the child, the less you have to worry about a wide selection of colours, or the provision of mixed colours. The small child works best with about three at a time.

Fig. 94 A small child paints *Pussy*

When he starts mixing his colours he could use a bun tin or plastic palette from an artists' store, into which he could mix powder and water from the spoons in the tin, rather than mess up the ready mixed paint in the containers.

Powder colours can be painted on any sort of paper, from kitchen or shelf paper to the thick absorbent sugar (construction) paper. It looks rather more colourful on the less absorbent papers, though children like to work on sugar (construction) paper as it has a softer feel. Powder colour can be mixed with other materials and still retain its colourful properties, i.e. mixed with sand for texture, mixed with cold water paste for finger

Fig. 95 *Monster in a dream* by a six year-old boy. One kind of painted excursion into imagination

painting, with plaster for the scratching technique of 'sgraffito', (see page 97) used thickly on papier-mâché texture it can cover imperfections.

Powder colour is highly applicable to the younger child who doesn't do much mixing because it quickly gets muddy if the paint is 'used' too much. It is a medium for direct handling, for contrasts of sharp colour, of pale and dark shades, rather than for close tonalities and subtlety of paint.

It is essential to provide five or six colours for the child's early painting days. These should be the three primary colours — blue, yellow and red — and black and white. The white will be necessary particularly for mixing purposes, as it can greatly enlarge the palette. Later yellow ochre could be added, as it mixes with black to velvety greens, and makes oranges and rich browns. Of the blues, ultramarine is the most useful.

From the reds and browns, raw umber, vermilion and crimson

A fox taking Helen. Marian and Paul for a ride.

Fig. 96 Another piece of imaginative play, by a pre-school age girl

lake can be chosen as the child progresses. On the whole, limit the colours to this brief list, unless the child specifically asks for a certain colour that he can't mix.

Poster colour is a finer mix, bought ready-made in jars or squat tins, and is widely used in secondary schools. They are expensive, though, and can harden if the lids are left off, or go mouldy if left damp for a long period with the lid on. They are not as hardy as powder paints although their transparent colour is capable of a fair amount of mixing without going muddy.

Tempera blocks can be bought in jars or flat plastic containers, and are a good buy for the junior school child. They have the brilliance of powder colour with the intermixing properties of poster paint. They are less messy to mix and require less getting ready before painting. Some children, however, prefer to use powder colour as they like the way it mixes. I have said that powder paint is better for an infant and tempera colour better for a school age child, suggesting that a change of technique is necessary. It will only be necessary if the child indicates it, perhaps because of things he is used to doing at school, or if you think he might like to try something new, in which case buy only a few until he makes his choice.

Watercolour, to be a satisfying medium, has to be used by an older child, who can learn how to handle it. Elaborate gift boxes are available with too many colours (usually in pans or

Fig. 97

cakes) and not enough paint and children are given these by doting relatives thinking they are doing them a favour. A small set of watercolour *tubes* would do the child more good, because he could set out on a palette or plate the amount of colour he needs for a picture. The big boxes of pans or cakes of colour go hard quickly, and the resultant mix with water is pale and anaemic next to the intensity a child can get with the tubes.

Paper Masks

Small children find that masks from paper bags or cardboard boxes give quick results and are easier than using papier-mâché. Large paper bags, wool or cloth scraps, or odd textures to be stuck on, glue, scissors, paints and colourless varnish are necessary to make these.

The features are painted on large and simple; textures such as paper, absorbent cotton raffia or wool can be stuck on for hair, eyebrows, teeth, collar etc. A nose made out of a triangle of paper can be added.

Cut out small shapes for eyes, nose and mouth, or just eyes and a slit for the nose. Tie elastic to both sides in the case of the cardboard box, so that the mask stays on. The bag mask goes over the head (see fig. 63).

Paper Sculpture

All kinds of forms can be made with paper, always allowing that two sides of a piece of folded paper should be the same shape, plus a length to join the two loose edges. Birds, insects, even houses can be made.

To make an insect, fold a piece of paper lengthways. Draw along it lines to indicate the head, thorax and abdomen (fig. 98). There are between two and four million different kinds of insects,

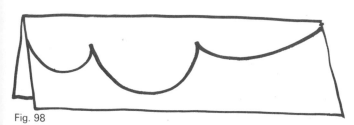

Fig. 98

so your species will be passable whatever you do. Cut out your shape in two thicknesses leaving the fold on one side. Add legs, wings, big eyes and perhaps antennae. Insects are symmetrical and any design painted on one wing should be repeated on the other. A retaining band of paper could be stuck or stapled on the underneath to join the two sides.

Papier-Mâché

Mix a paste from flour and water, boil until it is as thick as heavy pancake batter, making sure there are no lumps. Over a knot of crumpled and tightly squeezed newspaper stick two inch square pieces of paper coated in paste. Build up a thick layer of paper to the shape required. Large shapes can be built up by using other things as a base; balloons and jars. A large head could be made by the above method with the help of a blown-up balloon coated in warm vaseline and then covered with papier mâché. The balloon can be deflated when the papier mâché is dry.

Another way of making papier-mâchié is to soak newspapers overnight in a bucket of wallpaper paste. The paper should then be kneaded and torn very small, and the glue completely squeezed through it and absorbed. This can be used somewhat like clay.

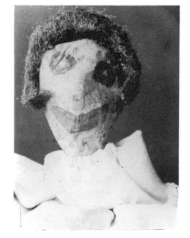

Fig. 99

To make a puppet head, take a tube the size of three fingers, either of cardboard or a length of thick plasticine (fig. 99). Put a few small pieces of dry newspaper round the tube and begin laying on papier-mâché. This is an 'adding to' technique and it is better to put features such as nose and ears on to the shape, rather than attempt to pull away the surrounding paper. Make the puppet head recognisable, with features. The neck must be definite, and a ridge made at the bottom for clothes to be sewn round. Hands can be made in exactly the same way, very simply moulded over a tube of greased plasticine the size of one finger. Hands should have a ridge at the wrist to allow cuffs to be sewn on.

When finished and dry, the heads can be painted in powder paints and afterwards varnished. Any extras such as hair and beards should be added later by sticking them on. Where a plasticine tube has been used it is slid out or taken out with a teaspoon.

Paste

Flour paste can be made by mixing smoothly flour and water, then adding more water and heating until thick and creamy. This paste can form the basis of finger paint, with the addition of powder colours. The same paste, to a different consistency, makes a modelling dough, which will keep well if wrapped in plastic.

Cold water paste can be bought from hardware, paint and decorators stores, as a powder to be mixed with water. It usually comes in pound and half-pound sizes. Wallpaper paste is stocked by decorators. It is good, but a little expensive.

Pastels

Pastels are like wax crayons to look at. Many are sold with a paper wrap at the end which is removed as the crayon wears down. The texture of pastel is chalky. A dust comes off it and all drawings need to be fixed with a shellac spray fixative to avoid smudging. Colours in pastels have a chalky quality and are seldom intense.

Oil pastels, where the chalk base is bound with oil, invariably sell in a paper wrap. These are a good buy for a child, as they are fairly cheap, in good colours, and are easy to use, being of a smooth, much less dusty texture than ordinary pastels.

Fig. 100 Drawing using pastels. A 'painting' with oil pastels is shown on page 35, Fig. 38

Plaster

Plaster of Paris can be bought in bags of up to seven pounds weight from many chemists in Great Britain, and in larger amounts at artists' stores, hardware and paint stores in the U.S.A.

To make up the dry powder you need a pail with water in it proportionate to the amount you need. The plaster is then added in spoonfuls, until the mound it makes stands above the water in the centre. Stir until it is creamy and let it stand for a little while to thicken to custard consistency before using.

Fig. 101 Bowl of plaster ready to mix

Fig. 102 Frame from a plaster tile, on greaseproof paper made with lolly sticks with plasticine stuck on the corners

Many things can be done with plaster but keep in mind that it is a liquid and needs to be contained—a box or tin lid, or a circular wall of plasticine on greaseproof paper would do. Besides being liquid it sticks to things, so anything it touches which you're going to need again needs to be thoroughly greased. It sticks to everything in fact except dry plaster. Once a plaster sculpture is dry it is impossible for any addition to adhere to it: it may seem to at first, but will crack off later.

And lastly—it hardens very quickly. Never wash plaster down the sink or toilet, which will clog; let unused plaster harden and then discard it.

Plaster Carving

For carving all that's needed is a block of plaster. This can be made by pouring the thick mixture into a shoe-box or smaller deep box. The box will disintegrate by the time the plaster has begun to set, so it should be tied round firmly, but not tightly, before the operation begins.

If a tin is used it should be well greased, as rust sets in quickly and plaster readily absorbs the rust colour. Similarly if wire is used with plaster it must be covered with plaster before it rusts, or use plastic covered wire. All knives or tools used with plaster should be washed carefully and quickly after use.

When the block has set it can be carved with a penknife or small chisel. A penknife is perhaps safer, unless some way of holding the block quite rigid is contrived, in which case a mallet and chisel can be used. Either way the plaster will be fairly slow to work away, unless you need to chip off large chunks. Plaster carving is a technique of slow erosion, compared with carving block salt or soap, where the going is extremely fast.

Plaster Casting

Casting is a way of reproducing in plaster a shape which is made in a soft material, such as plasticine or clay.

A plaster cast of a flat clay tile, for example, is simply made by greasing the clay tile, putting a tall clay wall round it, and pouring wet plaster over. When the plaster has dried it can be lifted by removing the clay retaining wall and pulling up the plaster block. The clay tile should come out easily, leaving its shape imprinted in the plaster, which is now your negative from which the actual tiles are made. By painting the dry plaster negative with warm vaseline and pouring new plaster into it one can obtain a new tile, in plaster. It should tip out when dry, as will others if the greasing is adequate, because plaster shrinks as it dries.

Casting is complex, however, and good results are never guaranteed. Only the older child, or one who is capable of sustained effort, should ever attempt it.

Plaster Reliefs with Sand or Clay Negative

For this you need a container like the lid of a garbage can or an old cake tin, plaster of Paris, fine sand from the sandpit, and a tablespoon.

Turn the lid of the dustbin upside down and wedge it firmly with a brick on each side of the handle. Fill the lid or cake pan level with damp sand. Add enough water so that the sand when shaped with the tablespoon stays in place.

This method enables one to make plaster tiles, round shapes, flowers, etc., and because the lid is deep in the centre one can sculpt quite deeply into the sand. Into the scooped-out shape (remembering that this is the negative) spoon the custard-thick plaster, making sure that the sides of the sand don't collapse, then the rest can be poured in. Leave the plaster overnight, and when quite dry turn it out. Any sand still adhering can be washed off, using a nail brush.

Fig. 103 Once a satisfactory scoop out has been made from the sand in the lid, put in the thickening plaster with a spoon at first to avoid spoiling the sides.

Fig. 104 Cleaning off the sand

Plaster Sculpture on a Wire Base

To a piece of wood heavy enough to take the weight of the finished sculpture without letting it topple, fix the end of a roll of garden wire, with a staple, nail or drawing pin. A six-foot length of baling wire is ample to construct a figure. Wind the wire in small circles and attach again, close to the other pin, thus making a foot. Pull the wire up to half the height of the figure which is to be made and loop down to the base again, fixing with a pin. Form the second foot in the same way as the other. These are then the legs. Wind the wire tightly up the leg and make a torso head and arms, coming down the body again and down the single wire leg to strengthen it.

Fig. 105 Clothing the wire skeleton with plaster

This little figure can be embellished in all manner of ways — with plaster for a face, wool or absorbent cotton hair and a moustache in black felt, holding a gun in each hand and a plaster holster belt around his hips. He can be completely covered in plaster — clothing on the wire skeleton, and features drawn on him can be covered lightly with wool or fabric, with plaster put on as a jacket while the plaster is soft. But whichever decision is made, the plaster sets quickly and allows few changes of mind. See Wire Frame Modelling.

Plaster Sgraffito

For this technique of picture making in plaster you will need two bowls, plaster and water, coloured ink, and a tool for scratching the plaster when it has set.

Into a box lid, or tin lid, oblong and fairly shallow, pour some custard-thick plaster into which coloured ink has been stirred. When that has set, add to the top, a thin layer of ordinary white plaster. While this is drying, an outline drawing of the subject—animal, figure or whatever—can be cut out of paper. When the plaster is dry enough the paper can be laid on to it and an outline scratched into the top layer of plaster. The shape can then be cut down to the coloured plaster so that the subject is coloured, or the surrounding area could be cut away down to the coloured plaster leaving the subject white.

This technique is very good for taking prints, particularly if the subject is the raised part of the plaster.

Plasticine

Plasticine is an oily clay, with a characteristic smell. It is not permanent, but as it doesn't dry out it is a good medium for use by small children, and older ones too. It sticks to almost everything, so it can be used over a wire frame to make a model of a figure. Plasticine models can be cast in plaster if the child wishes to keep his work permanently.

Potato Cuts See page 76.

Printing onto Paper from a Block

Put the block onto newspaper. Anything can be used for applying the printing ink as long as it is completely flat and non-absorbent; a tile, a piece of linoleum, an old mirror, or even a piece of greaseproof or wax paper folded round a table mat and securely stuck down. On this surface, roll the ink out flat with a rubber roller. Put the roller on to the block and roll the ink on evenly.

Lay the roller down carefully on the newspaper and transfer the block to a piece of paper. Make sure hands are clean. Put the paper for printing over the block. Press over the block with the finger tips, taking care not to let it slip on the ink. Take a table-

Fig. 106 Little equipment is necessary for printing

spoon and with the rounded surface press it with circular movements over the paper. If the paper is fairly thin you should be able to see that the ink is printing on to your top paper. Spoon all over including corners and edges. Lift a corner to see how the ink is printing. When the print is all right all over pull the paper off and leave to dry.

The paper should be fairly thin to be sure of an even print. Newsprint or shelf paper is better than most heavier types of paper.

Cleanliness is obviously important. If when you've finished spooning your fingers are inky, the paper can be taken off the block by first putting a small piece of card between your thumb and fingers and using it as a clip over the edge of the paper.

A print can be made by any variation on either the 'adding' or 'taking away' methods. The materials which can be put on to a block, stuck on, inked and printed are too numerous to list. Anything flat that one can see has printing potential, from a

Fig. 107 First the lino block is inked

Figs. 108 and 109 Then the paper laid on the block is rubbed with a spoon to ink every part. Looking at the print

rusty piece of iron to a haphazard group of dead matches stuck down. It matters less what is used to make the print than that the child is learning about textures and line. Feathers, leaves, fabrics, patterned glass, wire mesh, crinkly and silver paper, corrugated card are all objects which can be cut or otherwise used to place on a base of cardboard, lino-tile or hardboard for printing. Once the things needed for the printing surface are collected, the child decides where they should be placed on the board, and they're then stuck to the block base with a good contact glue.

When different things are placed on the block and inked one must be sure that they are properly stuck and will not move. Sometimes the ink goes straight into absorbent materials, like balsa wood, strawboard and fabrics, and will not print properly. Put ink on and let it dry. This gives a firm coating and seals the surface. It should then print if all the objects are reasonably the same height and do not slip about.

For the 'taking away' method of printmaking, the top of whatever you are using will be printed, and what is cut away will be white. So if a child cuts away a line shape of something he should realise that it will print as a white line on a black shape. Linoleum or cork tile (not the plastic type) can be cut easily with a lino-cutting tool or a knife. Cardboard, strawboard or balsa need not always be cut, but can have shapes pressed into them. Pastry cutters, bottle tops, fork dents, wire mesh imprints can all be pressed into them.

Harder surfaces, like plywood, plank wood and veneer boards are slightly more difficult to use technically, but are very rewarding to use as the grain is the starting point of the picture. If the as yet unused wood could be printed before anything is done to it, an idea for design may emerge from looking at the print. If the grain swirls, then let the cut be a swirling one.

Puppets See pages 55 and 77.

Rubbings from Brass

For rubbings from wood, brick, glass, etc., see page 66.

You need; white lining paper sold in decorators' shops, 'heelball' a tallow and beeswax mixture used by shoe menders and bought from them in cakes in size up to about four inches across.

It must be stressed that permission to take rubbings of brasses in churches must be requested before one sets out if possible, from the vicar or verger. Sometimes they may ask for a small payment.

Make sure that the brass plate is free from grit, by gently rubbing down. Lay the paper over it, ideally with a second person holding it to make sure it remains smooth and unrucked throughout the process, or keep the paper firm with weights or smooth stones. Work from left to right with round movements of the heelball ensuring an even depth of colour over the design, and checking the paper is going over the incisions in the brass plate, showing as white lines on the paper.

Different textures of heelball can be bought. The softest kind will make an even black where there are large patches of brass to be covered. The hardest heelball will be best where the brass plate is of very intricate design.

Scraperboard See Wax Scraperboard.

Stained Glass Effect

Cut out black cardboard to a design then cut out with a sharp knife, removing shapes whose spaces will be filled in with coloured tissue, and leaving black slats wide enough to glue on the tissue paper.

Place the cut-out cardboard over the tissue at the relevant shape, and lightly draw round in soft pencil. Cut the tissue paper to shape leaving a quarter inch all round for sticking. Fix the 'stained glass' with glue taking care to disperse the colours all over to achieve a balance. Colours can be intensified by using

Fig. 110

two or three layers of tissue, or changed by mixing, or overlaying, one colour on top of another. Then hang in a window to let light through.

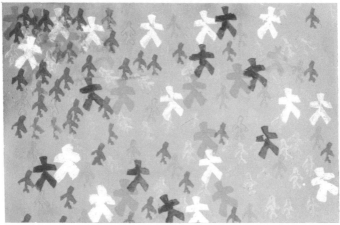

Fig. 111

Stick Printing

These little men (fig. 111) are all from one stamp made from

101

cutting a simple figure into the flat end of a cylindrical scrap of wood. Three eleven year-olds worked on one picture, with a different coloured ink for each group of figures. The project was to indicate by the direction and position of the figures what their team would do when the third group, the 'baddies', infiltrated the picture from one corner. The same kind of print could be made from a cut potato.

Textures

Listed here are a few of the many textures and 'found objects' which can be used for picture-making or other visual experience: stones, pebbles—keep different colours apart; twigs; leaves; sea weed; shells; driftwood; cork; buttons; beads; cocktail sticks; bottle tops; straws; wire bits; egg boxes; toilet roll holders; small fragments of glass, mirrors and coloured stones; tiny bits of broken crockery; rice; lentils; dried peas; barley; kidney beans; butter beans; macaroni and spaghetti shells; dried melon seeds.

Some of these things have a natural place in the food cupboard. The children could make a chest of drawers out of cardboard for keeping their collections; a grocery box can be used, with handkerchief tissue boxes stacked as drawers, neatly labelled.

Tie-dyeing

Tie and dye is an easy method of making a design on fabric. The cloth is knotted or tied round tightly with string. Where the string is tight the dye bath into which the tied fabric is put won't

Fig. 112 Tying with buttons and seeds is only necessary if a large motif is wanted, otherwise just string or thread is enough

Fig. 113 Material untied and spread flat; this is a pattern made by tying

penetrate. Rinse the material after dyeing and untie and open out to dry. It is not necessary to include objects in the tied up fabric, although buttons and cotton reels (spools) are being used in the photograph (fig. 112). The tie begins with a good, tight slip knot.

Wax Resist See Batik Printing.

Wax Scraperboard

With coloured wax crayons, some cardboard no larger than postcards, and a nail or knitting needle, a colourful picture can be made. Using a different coloured wax crayon for each layer, build up several overall layers of wax on the card. Finish with dark brown or black. The picture is revealed in the scraping down to the layer which contains the colour needed. Laborious, but absorbing to an older child.

This is a kind of scraperboard or scratchboard technique, but it is cheaper and contains colour. Artists' scraperboard is specially prepared with fine chalk and overlaid with a layer of soft black; lines are scraped or engraved out of the black to the white beneath, making a white on black drawing.

Wire Frame Modelling

For this are needed some flexible or plastic coated wire, pliers, a lolly or ice cream stick and plaster.

A child can get quite a stable wire frame by fixing wire on to a small piece of wood by laying an end of wire to the wood block and securing it with a metal staple. Wire can then be twisted into the desired shape, an armature or framework for a figure or animal. The wire is a skeleton, over which the muscles and limbs will be shaped in plaster. The wire is necessary to support the legs and arms.

For working in this direct kind of way plaster must be getting thick. With the lolly or ice cream stick apply the plaster to the wire frame. Work must be done quickly, because wet plaster will not stick to dry. It the plaster dries before the model is finished should be thoroughly soaked with water, brushed or sponged on, before work continues. Once hardened plaster should not be worked over, but when rewetted will take another layer on top of it. See Plaster Sculpture on a Wire Base.

For further reading

Creative Print Making by Peter Green. Batsford, London.
Watson-Guptill, New York.

One Piece of Paper by Michael Grater. Mills and Boon, London.
Taplinger, New York.

Simple Printmaking by Cyril Kent and Mary Cooper.
Studio Vista, London. Watson-Guptill, New York.

Tie and Dye as a Present Day Craft by Anne Maile.
Mills and Boon, London. Taplinger, New York.

What Children Scribble and Why by Rhoda Kellog.
National Press, Palo Alto, California.